NUTSHELL
GROWING GRAPES

Everything you need to know in a nutshell

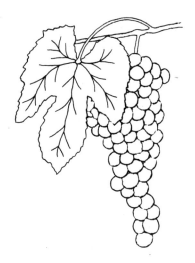

Clive Simms

Other titles by Clive Simms in the
Nutshell Guide to Growing series:

Walnuts
Figs
Blueberries, Cranberries & Lingonberries
Hazelnuts

Text © Clive Simms 2005
Illustrations © Sam Taylor 2005
Reprinted 2006

Published by:
Orchard House Books,
Woodhurst, Essendine,
Stamford, Lincs. PE9 4LQ
Tel: 01780 755615

www.orchardhousebooks.com

ISBN 0-9544607-2-3

Contents

Introduction

Grapevines are often perceived as difficult tender plants that require lots of specialised knowledge in order to grow them. This beginner's guide will show this is untrue! Not only are vines fully hardy throughout Britain, but their cultivation requires only very basic, and easily learnt, skills.

Although grapes are popularly associated with large scale commercial vineyards, good crops of fruit can also be produced from just one or two vines in the garden.

You can grow your own grapes for fresh eating, juice or winemaking almost as easily as growing gooseberries.

Site

The warmer and sunnier the spot the more easily grapevines will ripen their crop. As Britain often lacks such conditions the ideal place to grow them is under glass. An unheated **greenhouse** allows a wide range of grapes to be grown, while a heated greenhouse extends the choice even further, making even very late ripening cultivars possible.

When grown **outdoors** in the open garden the site must be as warm and sheltered as possible. In general, the area south of a line from southern Wales to the Wash is suitable for outdoor vines. In this situation the choice of grapevine is crucial as only the earlier ripening cultivars are likely to be successful when grown outdoors in the UK (see pages 36-38).

Those living in unfavourable areas could utilise a spot against a **sunny wall** or **fence**. Growing under high cloches (45cm high minimum) is an advantage in cooler areas.

Sites prone to late frosts may require the vines to be covered on chilly nights in spring to protect the new growth and flowers.

Vines need a well-drained soil with a neutral pH of around 7. Poor, infertile soils are no problem, they are better than very fertile ones, but poor drainage is fatal to vines.

Potted vines may be grown where garden space is limited. Even a south-facing balcony is a potential site for growing grapes.

Feeding and watering

Newly planted vines require regular thorough soakings to encourage their roots to grow deep into the soil. This is particularly important with sites at the base of a wall, which are notoriously dry. However, once established, vines have roots that go down deep into the soil so are able to find water and nutrients from a considerable depth.

Apply the water close to the ground to avoid wetting the foliage as this encourages leaf diseases. Discontinue watering in late summer to allow the vine to become fully dormant for the winter. Heavy watering, especially after prolonged drought, often results in the fruit splitting and spoiling.

Feed with care; too much fertiliser creates more problems than too little. Over feeding, particularly with nitrates, leads to excessive growth, poor fruit set, and risk of disease.

Inorganic growers usually apply a spring feed of a general-purpose fertiliser such as 'Growmore' at the rate of $66g/m^2$ plus $15g/m^2$ of sulphate of potash. An 8cm mulch of good compost or manure spread around the vine is also a good idea. Organic growers use nothing else, with excellent results.

Vines are particularly sensitive to lack of magnesium in the soil and will show this by chlorosis, or yellowing, of the leaves. Correct by spraying with a solution of 115g of magnesium sulphate per 5 litres of water plus a little soft soap. Repeat at two-week intervals until re-greening takes place. A spring dressing of $66g/m^2$ of magnesium sulphate per plant prevents future problems.

Pollination

Wild grapevines are usually male or female plants, but almost all cultivated grapevines are self-fertile and set fruit by themselves.

flowers

During flowering stroke the flower clusters with your cupped hands to spread the pollen around and improve pollination. Fruit set on greenhouse vines is better if the atmosphere is on the dry side during the flowering period. Poor pollination results in both large and very small fruit, often called 'hen and chickens'.

Seedless grapes don't require pollination. Traditionally they have been grown for drying to make currants and sultanas, but more recently new seedless cultivars have been bred specifically for dessert fruit.

Pruning

Uncertainty about pruning and training probably deters many people from planting vines, but the basic principles involved are simple and easy to learn. Although there are many different ways to manage grapevines all seek to influence the vine to produce regular crops of good quality grapes.

Pruning should be carried out in December or January during the dormant season. If pruning is delayed until early spring vines are prone to bleed sap from the pruning cuts.

The vine's growing shoots are referred to as either **leaders** or **laterals**. Put simply, leaders are the stems that lead the way the vine is growing, and laterals are the side shoots that grow out from these leaders. A strong one year old leader may also be referred to as a **cane.** The shoots that arise from a lateral shoot are called **sub-laterals**.

Grapes produce fruit on the current year's new shoots. These shoots grow from buds on the stem of the previous year's growth. These fruit buds may be found along the entire length of the previous year's growth or be restricted to further along the shoot.

Therefore, there are two basic ways of pruning grapes, **spur** or **cane** pruning.

Spur pruning is best suited to cultivars derived from the European grape (*Vitis vinifera*), which tend to have their fruit buds near the base of the previous year's growth as well as further along. European grapes may also be cane pruned if desired.

11

Spur pruning is probably the easiest pruning method for amateurs to understand. All you need to do is reduce the extension growth of the leader by about half and prune back the lateral shoots to one bud every winter. After spur pruning the leader is often referred to as a **rod** or **cordon**.

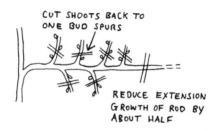

CUT SHOOTS BACK TO ONE BUD SPURS

REDUCE EXTENSION GROWTH OF ROD BY ABOUT HALF

spur pruning a lateral shoot

By allowing more than one leader to develop, either horizontally or vertically, this rod and spur system of management may be used to train the vine over arches and arbours, or form a permanent framework to fill spaces on walls. Leave 1m between the vertical rods and 0.5m between horizontal ones to avoid congestion.

Cane pruning, also called Guyot pruning, is the best way to prune vines derived from American grape species (*Vitis labrusca, rupestris, riparia & aestivalis*) that have fruit buds some distance away from the shoot base. The old fruiting branch is pruned away and replaced annually. This means a new shoot must be grown specifically as a replacement cane every year, in a similar way to growing summer fruiting raspberries.

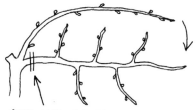

PULL DOWN NEW REPLACEMENT CANE

CUT OUT OLD FRUITING CANE COMPLETELY

cane pruning

Training

Grapevines are climbing plants and require support as they grow, which means fixing something to a house wall, garden fence or inside a greenhouse to provide a point of attachment. To grow grapes in the open garden it's best to construct a trellis of stout supports and tensioned wires on which to train them, as described in the next chapter.

Vines have tendrils and will happily cling on to any support themselves. However, tendrils can be a nuisance and they may be removed and the shoots tied in place with raffia or soft string.

Greenhouse: Plant the vine inside or outside the greenhouse, whichever is more convenient. If planted outside, a hole will have to be made for the stem to pass through. Remember to make a hole big enough to allow the vine to grow in girth! It's then trained along supporting wires at the side of the greenhouse or up and along the ridge. In both cases make sure that 30cm is left between the vine's leaves and the glass to allow good air circulation and prevent shoots pressing against the glass and scorching.

Greenhouse vines are often trained on the rod and spur system (see pages 12 & 23) to give a compact plant that's easy to keep in order, but they may also be cane pruned if preferred (see pages 13 & 24).

Walls and fences: These need to have wires or a strong supporting frame fixed in place leaving a 4cm gap behind. This is fairly easy to do on a wooden fence, but to fix wires to a brick or stone wall use wooden battens with metal 'vine eyes' every 2m. This enables the wires to be attached securely and pulled tight.

vine eyes

Open garden: If a sturdy pole is driven into the ground the vine can be trained to form a single fruiting cordon, or a standard. The latter has a bare stem crowned by several fruit-bearing branches.

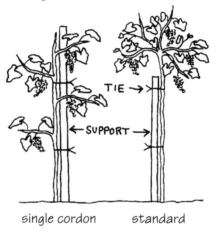

TIE →

← SUPPORT →

single cordon   standard

Using several poles or canes allows more ambitious training to be attempted such as a double 'U' shaped cordon or a fan shape. Alternatively, you could construct a trellis.

A simple two wire trellis

Many different trellis systems exist but the simplest is the **two-wire trellis**. To construct this involves two wooden posts (treated to resist decay) approximately 7.5cm to 10cm diameter x 1.5m long being driven 50cm into the ground.

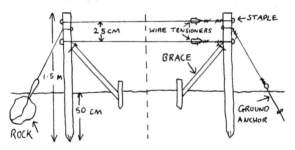

The posts may be vertical if braced, or splayed out at an angle for extra strength if anchored.

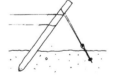

The posts should be placed 3m to 4m apart, which gives sufficient space for one or two vines. Obviously, a longer trellis requires more posts to prevent the wires sagging.

The posts must be absolutely secure and require bracing posts or ground anchors to prevent them being pulled towards one another when the wire is tensioned. If you have the space use both as a belt and braces approach!

Screw-in ground anchors may be bought from hardware stores, but a cheaper alternative is to loop strong wire to a large rock and bury it.

ground anchor

Next, fix the two support wires (heavy duty 12 gauge galvanised steel) 25cm apart to one post by running them through drilled holes and twisting the wire around itself to secure. Alternatively, loop the wire around the post then twist to secure and staple at the desired height.

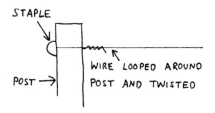

Never fix wires simply by stapling them to a post, the constant tension will eventually pull the staple out and your vine will end up on the ground!

The other end of each wire should be attached to the second post and tension applied to give rigidity to the structure. There are three ways of doing this:

1. Use purpose made **eye bolts** fixed through the post.

eye bolt

2. Attach a short length of **chain** to the wire and hook this over a nail in the post.

WIRE CHAIN

CHAIN PULLED TIGHT OVER A NAIL

tensioning a wire to a post using a length of chain

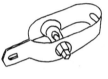

wire tensioner

3. Attach **ratchet wire tensioners** to the post with loops of wire. The support wire is then threaded through the open end and wound around the central spindle. Tension is applied using a spanner.

Short stretches of trellis may also be made from lengths of wood or rigid metal pipe instead of supporting wires. More ambitious trellis systems require taller posts and more wires than the basic two-wire type.

Training vines on a trellis

Once your trellis is complete, plant and train a young vine against it. Grow the vine up a cane until it reaches the support wires.

If growth is slow in the first year cut the vine back hard again the following winter to stimulate stronger growth next season. All low growing shoots should be protected from rabbit damage by surrounding them with wire mesh cylinders. Although rabbits don't appear too keen on the old woody growth they love to nibble tender green shoots.

Once growing strongly the vine may be trained against the trellis and spur pruned to form permanent fruiting arms, or cane pruned to give temporary fruiting arms that are replaced annually. The initial training is the same for both methods and the following three diagrams show how it's done.

21

Initial training

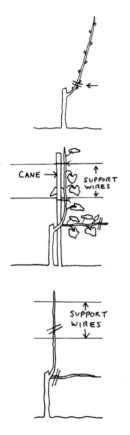

In winter prune the young vine back hard, leaving only two buds of the previous season's growth. This stimulates strong re-growth the next summer.

The following summer train the vine up a cane to reach the support wires. Nip out the growing tip of any lateral growths after five leaves.

In winter prune back the vertical growth to the height of the lower wire. Remove any lateral shoots below this height.

The next stage is to train the vine to have one or more fruiting arms. The arms may either become permanent features, often called **cordons** or **rods**, that are **spur pruned**, or the arms may be **cane pruned** and replaced annually after fruiting with **replacement canes** tied into place every year.

Training for spur pruning

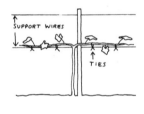

In summer train two shoots along the lower wire. The following winter reduce the arms by half and prune any laterals back to one bud.

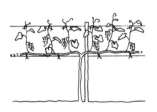

The following summer laterals from the two arms will fruit. Thin them to 30cm apart by pruning out any surplus. Tie them to the top wire to stop them falling over. In winter prune these laterals back to one bud spurs ready for fruiting again next year.

23

Training for cane pruning

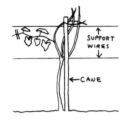

In summer allow three shoots to grow out and train them vertically up a stout cane. Pinch out any laterals after five leaves.

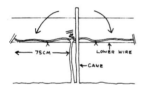

The following winter pull down two shoots and tie to the lower wire. Prune them back to around 75cm. The third shoot is pruned back to leave a three bud stump.

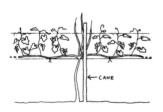

Next summer lateral shoots on the arms will fruit. Tie them to the top wire for support. Train three more shoots vertically from the three bud stump. In winter remove the fruited arms and replace with new canes. The third cane is cut back to a three bud stump to repeat the cycle.

Both spur and cane pruned vines should be allowed only one flower cluster per lateral shoot to set and develop fruit. Aim to have no more than one bunch of grapes per 30cm along the arm. Pinch out the growing tip two leaves after the fruit. Any non-fruiting laterals are pinched out after five leaves have formed.

summer pruning

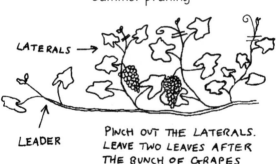

LATERALS →

LEADER

PINCH OUT THE LATERALS.
LEAVE TWO LEAVES AFTER
THE BUNCH OF GRAPES

Thereafter, throughout the summer, pinch back any subsequent re-growth to one leaf.

A grape arbour

One useful way of growing grapes is to use them to cover an arbour to make a delightful shady place to sit on a hot summer's day. Planting a vine that may be spur pruned is best in this situation.

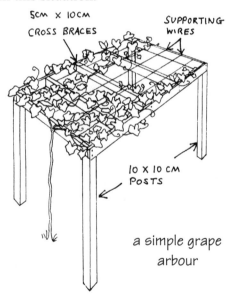

5CM × 10CM CROSS BRACES

SUPPORTING WIRES

10 X 10 CM POSTS

a simple grape arbour

Propagation

Grapevines may be easily propagated from hardwood cuttings taken in autumn and winter. Use sturdy pencil-thick material from the base of last season's growth. The length of the cuttings isn't critical. Make the basal cut immediately beneath a bud and insert into a pot of free draining potting compost. No heat or rooting hormone is required. Such cuttings will also root if placed in the ground outdoors.

Single bud or 'eye' cuttings may be made in spring. Press them horizontally onto the surface of the compost and keep at 21°C.

vine eyes

Take summer cuttings in late July or August and root in a heated propagator. Vines also layer quite easily if shoots are pegged down to the ground in spring or summer.

Grafted vines are often used in commercial vineyards because particular **rootstocks** may be advantageous for certain soil types or be tolerant of pests.

The most likely rootstock to be encountered by UK amateurs is called SO4. It increases the vigour and productivity of the vine in cold climates and copes well with heavy clay soils. Its' tolerance to the pest Phylloxera (see page 30) isn't an advantage to UK amateur growers as this pest doesn't occur here. Also, the authorities are likely to combat any future outbreak by destroying all vines in the affected area, grafted or not.

Vines are easily grown from pips, but the resulting seedling plants are variable and a large proportion will be disease prone, poor croppers, and possibly either male or female plants which wouldn't be self-fertile. Unless you're trying to raise new grape cultivars I'd leave seedlings alone.

Pests

- **Brown scale insect** (*Parthenolecanium corni*): Small (5mm) shell-like pests found attached to stems, shoots and leaves of both indoor and outdoor plants. Young insects ('crawlers') move around the plant before settling to feed on sap. Adults may be wiped off by brushing with soapy water. Spray the crawlers with insecticide when they are active in late spring/early summer.

- **Vine weevil** (*Otiorhynchus sulcatus*): The adult is a dull blackish brown insect with a prominent elongated snout. It's active at night feeding on leaves, causing notching on the leaf edges. However, the white larval grubs are the real problem as they eat the plant's roots. They have voracious appetites and are particularly fond of pots of rooted cuttings.

vine weevil

vine weevil
grub

Adult weevils may be collected at night when they're feeding and then destroyed. The grubs are usually dealt with by using a microscopic nematode worm as a biological control.

• **Vine phylloxera** (*Daktulosphaira vitifolie,* also called *Phylloxera vastatrix* and *Viteus vitifolie)*: This aphid-like insect was accidentally introduced to Europe from America in the 1860's and soon became a serious pest of commercial vineyards. Fortunately, it's never managed to establish itself in the UK... so far! It causes obvious round galls to form on the leaf surface, and root infestations may kill the entire plant unless resistant rootstocks are used (see page 28). Although unlikely to be encountered here it's a legally notifiable pest and any suspicious leaf galls should be immediately reported to the appropriate government authority responsible for plant health.

- **Red spider mite** (*Tetranychus urticae*): Tiny mites found on the underside of the leaves causing speckles on the upper surface.
- **Mealybugs** (*Pseudococcus obscurus*): 3mm long insects covered in white 'wool', usually found in the leaf axils.
- **Whitefly** (*Trialeurodes vaporariorum*): Tiny flies that cluster underneath the leaves. The eggs and young are difficult to kill by spraying.

All three pests above are commonly found on greenhouse vines and feed by sucking sap from the plant's leaves and stems. Insecticide may control them although biological control is often more convenient and effective. Mealybugs are killed by painting them with methylated spirit using a fine brush.

- **Birds and Wasps**: Both are major pests of ripening grapes. Foil them by enclosing the fruit bunches in wraps of frost protection fleece or muslin. Bags made from the legs of old nylon tights also work well. Secure in position with clothes pegs.

If your budget doesn't run to a walk-in fruit cage you can cover individual vines with fine mesh netting. Enclose the entire vine, or just fasten two strips of netting together to cover the fruit leaving tall shoots and leaves protruding. If necessary use notched sticks to push the net sides away from the grapes to make sure the birds can't peck through.

Birds may also be deterred for short periods of time by various techniques including reflective 'scare' tape, plastic owls or a radio tuned to music…

…or talk shows!

Diseases

The European grape (*Vitis vinifera*) is susceptible to three common fungal diseases, two of which have been accidentally imported from the USA. Native American species usually have a high degree of resistance to these diseases, so hybrids between European and American grapes frequently inherit this trait. These hybrids are a good choice for the amateur as they need much less preventative spraying.

- **Grey mould** (*Botrytis cinerea*): Occurs on both outdoor and greenhouse grapes and causes reduced fruit set and rotting of the fruit which becomes covered with a greyish brown fungal growth. It's worse in cool, wet seasons. Good ventilation which allows the vines to dry quickly after wetting helps, along with removing and destroying infected fruit to prevent the disease spreading.

- **Powdery mildew** (*Uncinula necator*): A common problem affecting both indoor and greenhouse grapes, especially when the soil is dry and the air circulation poor. The leaves and fruit become covered in a white powdery coating that causes extensive damage and spoils the grapes. Adequate ventilation and watering help prevent the problem. Dusting with sulphur or spraying with wettable sulphur according to the manufacturer's instructions is a good remedy. If the disease occurs every year begin routine dusting or spraying early before the symptoms show.

- **Downy mildew** (*Plasmopara viticola*): An occasional disease of outdoor grapes in Britain that causes pale yellow-green patches on the leaf surface. There are no suitable fungicides available to the amateur grower, but a good airflow around the vines reduces the risk of this disease. Organic growers maintain that applications of compost are a good preventative measure.

Buying your plant

Most garden centres and nurseries stock grapevines although the choice is usually limited. As the selection of an appropriate cultivar is crucial, particularly for vines planted outdoors, it's important to do your homework first and not simply buy what's on offer locally… it could make the difference between success and failure! This may mean you have to seek out stockists by referring to the **RHS Plant Finder** book, or the website at **www.rhs.org.uk** . The most important considerations are how early the fruit ripens, and how prone the vine is to disease.

As there are over 200 grape cultivars available in the UK the following list is confined to those most suitable for amateur growers wishing to grow dessert or wine grapes outdoors or in an unheated greenhouse.

Aurore (Seibel 5279): European/American hybrid grape. Very early ripening white fruit. Wine or dessert. Spur or cane prune.

Black Hamburgh: European black dessert grape. Very late ripening so best in a greenhouse. Spur or cane prune.

Boskoop Glory: (**Glory of Boskoop**) Hybrid European/American black dessert grape. Ripens late. Spur or cane prune.

Brandt: European/American hybrid. Small, black late ripening dessert fruit. Commonly grown for the red autumn leaves. Spur prune.

Glenora Seedless: American dessert grape. Ripens mid-season. Delicious black fruit and red leaves in autumn. Cane prune.

Himrod Seedless: American dessert grape. Golden yellow berries, early ripening. Cane prune.

Maréchal Foch and **Maréchal Joffre**: Both are vigorous, disease free, very early ripening European/American hybrids. Blue-black grapes. Wine or dessert. Cane prune.

Muscat Bianca: (**Vitalis Gold**) Vigorous disease resistant European/American hybrid. Yellow fruit ripens mid-season. Dessert or wine. Spur or cane prune.

Muscat Bleu: (**Vitalis Ruby**) Blue dessert European/American hybrid. Ripens late. Leaves colour well in autumn. Spur or cane prune.

Phoenix: European/American hybrid. White muscat flavoured grapes. Ripens late. Wine or dessert. Cane prune.

Pirovano 14: European/American hybrid. Early ripening dark red/black fruit. Dessert or wine. Leaves colour well in autumn. Spur or cane prune.

Schuyler: (pronounced Sky-ler) Early ripening European/American black grape. Dessert or wine. Red autumn colour. Spur or cane prune.

Siegerrebe: Very early ripening European grape. Tawny-gold fruit with slight muscat flavour. Dessert or wine. Spur or cane prune.

Suffolk Red Seedless: American grape. Disease resistant and early ripening. Dessert. Cane prune.

Triomphe D'Alsace: (**Triomphe**) Black European/American hybrid grape. Vigorous and disease resistant. Ripens mid-season. Wine or dessert. Spur or cane prune.

Queen of Esther: European/American hybrid grape. Mildew resistant blue/black grapes. Dessert or wine. Spur or cane prune.

Harvesting

As your grapes ripen they will become softer
and sweeter. They'll also take on their
characteristic colour that may range from
pale translucent yellow, green, red, blue to
jet-black. Many grapes have a thin whitish
waxy coating or 'bloom'
on their skin that is
damaged by touching.
Not only does this bloom
look attractive,
particularly if you're
exhibiting at the local
produce show, but it also helps to shed
rainwater and prevent mould.

Don't pick the fruit as soon as it looks ripe. It
tastes better if it's left to 'finish' or hang on
the vine for some time longer to allow the
sugar content to increase. The time taken for
this to happen varies with the type of grape

and the weather, but when the fruit tastes sweet enough harvest your crop. Greenhouse grapes may be left on the vine for a little longer than those grown outdoors if a cool dry atmosphere is maintained.

The Victorians used to place bunches of grapes, complete with a short woody stem, in bottles of water containing pieces of charcoal. They were angled to prevent the bunches from touching the bottles and left in a cool dark room where they would keep for some time. A modern way to store grapes is to freeze the fruit in helping sized amounts to thaw and use as topping on ice cream or yoghurt.

Freshly picked grapes are not only delicious but rich in vitamins and antioxidants too. Enjoy them straight from the vine, make juice for a refreshing drink, or stock up the cellar with your very own house wine!